MW00624071

HEAVENLY TREASURE

Robert Abel

Valentine Publishing House
Denver, Colorado

Valentine Publishing House LLC
P.O. Box 27422
Denver, Colorado 80227

The Scripture quotations contained herein are from the New Revised Standard Version Bible: Catholic Edition copyright © 1993 and 1989 by the Division of Christian Education of the National Council of the Churches of Christ in the U.S.A. Used by permission. All rights reserved.

Cover Graphics—Desert Isle Design LLC

Publisher's Cataloging-in-Publication Data

Abel, Robert.
    Heavenly Treasure / Robert Abel — 2nd ed.

        p. : ill. ; cm.

    ISBN–10: 0-9796331-3-3
    ISBN–13: 978-0-9796331-3-3
    Includes bibliographical references.

1. Catholic Church. 2. Church renewal—Religious aspects—Christianity.
3. Stewardship—Religious aspects—Christianity. I. Title.

BX1746 .A24 2009
282

Printed in the United States of America.

"See, I am coming soon; my reward is with me,
to repay according to everyone's work.
I am the Alpha and the Omega,
the first and the last,
the beginning and the end."

Revelation 22:12–13

FOREWORD

It is with great pleasure that I draft the foreword to *Heavenly Treasure* because of the pressing urgency of serious need in many African nations. After experiencing a dramatic spike in food and commodity prices, many families, particularly those living in rural areas, are in dire need. It is estimated that six million children will die this year from malnutrition before their fifth birthday. Many of these infants will pass away quietly in the most remote areas, far removed from the scrutiny and conscience of the international community.

In East Africa, one of the poorest regions south of the Sahara, millions of children are suffering from malaria and other water-borne diseases. Almost half the population—some 75 million people lack access to safe drinking water. To make matters worse, the rampant AIDS epidemic has been robbing families of wage earners and communities of leaders, leaving millions of orphans in its wake. Other areas are still trying to recover from drought and war-torn economics, while post-election violence claims even more lives.

Due to the extreme urgency of these and other pressing needs, a request from every parish in America is inevitable. It is my greatest hope that every Catholic community in America will reach out to form a ministry partnership with African pastors. There are many excellent ministry opportunities that can be supervised by dedicated deacons and pastors, in exchange for the opportunity to earn a vast amount of heavenly treasure.

✠ Most Reverend Philip A S Anyolo
Bishop of Homa Bay Diocese
Kenya, East Africa

CHAPTER ONE

The situation seemed so hopeless that I threw all my money into the church collection basket early Sunday morning. I only had $287 to my name and needed $713 to make my first mortgage payment. I felt too ashamed to ask my parents for help, because they didn't want me to buy the house in the first place. None of my friends would loan me $500, so with nowhere else to turn, I decided to give God a try.

As the usher passed the basket in front of me, I said a prayer while slowly releasing my grip. The roll of cash fell from my hand into what seemed like an eternal moment. As the church service progressed, I couldn't stop thinking about the little red house in northwest Denver. I had purchased the property about a month earlier with the intention of building an apartment in the basement.

The house had three bedrooms upstairs and a back door that led down a set of stairs into the basement. All I needed to do was build a wall to separate the kitchen from the back door, and I would have a three-bedroom unit upstairs that would rent for $550. After building another three-bedroom unit in the basement that rented for $480, I would have positive cash flow on the property.

Everything was going according to plan, until the day I knocked on the front door to collect the rent. The lady who answered looked at me with indignation and said, "What do you want?"

"I'm here to collect the rent," I said.

"We're not going to pay you, because you are making too much noise in the basement."

Her words hit me so hard that I took a step back and almost fell off the porch. Not knowing what to say, I blurted out, "Well, if you don't pay me, I'm going to evict you!"

"Go ahead," she said. "It will take you six months to get us out of here!" Then she slammed the door.

I desperately needed my tenants' rent money. I had spent my entire life savings on closing costs. I had been spending my weekly paychecks on gas for my truck and construction materials for the basement. I had intentionally saved $287, because that, combined with the rent money, would be enough for me to make my first mortgage payment.

The thought of fighting with my tenants in court for the next six months was even more dreadful. The only alternative I could think of was turning to God. As least if things didn't work out, I would have someone to blame besides myself.

A few hours after I threw all my money into the church collection basket, I received a phone call from my tenants. "You had better get down here! Your clothes dryer burned up our laundry. Firemen kicked in the front door. Now we're really going to sue you!"

Immediately, I ran to my vehicle and drove as fast as possible to see what was going on. When I arrived, the fire truck was pulling away. My harvest yellow clothes dryer was sitting in the front yard, only now it was harvest yellow and black.

As I entered the house, the tenants were packing boxes. "What's going on now?" I asked.

"We're moving," the man said.

The smoke damage was unbearable. The stench of burned plastic made my eyes water after being inside for only a few minutes.

The next day, I called my insurance company to set an appointment with the adjuster, and by the time he arrived, the tenants had already vacated the property. After looking around the house for a few minutes, the adjuster started taking measurements. He calculated how much it would cost to repair the front door and fix several windows that the firemen had broken. He also calculated the cost for washing the walls and replacing the dryer. When all the numbers were added together he said, "How does $2,800 sound?"

"Wow! That would be great," I said.

"Very good," The adjuster said as he wrote me a check.

A few hours later, another man knocked on the front door and said, "Hi, my name is Don. I'm a public insurance adjuster. Do you mind if I come in?"

"You're too late," I said. "I already settled with my insurance company."

"Do you mind if I look at the numbers?" Don said.

I handed Don the paperwork, and after looking it over, he said, "They should have given you enough to repaint the walls, not just wash them. If you want, I will get you a better settlement."

Don was only charging a 10 percent commission on the extra money that he collected, so after reviewing his paperwork, I signed his contract. Within a week, Don had come up with an additional $2,000.

I was overjoyed. After I had thrown all my money into the church collection basket, God had successfully evicted the tenants and put several thousand dollars in my pocket. All I needed to do was buy a used dryer and repaint the kitchen walls. The smoke smell disappeared after I left the windows open for a week, and I even managed to make my mortgage payment within the grace period.

CHAPTER TWO

$

After experiencing the miracle-working power of God, I started to give tithing some very serious consideration. In my research, I came across a quote from Malachi 3:8–10, where the entire nation of Israel was under a curse because they failed to present a full tithe to the Lord:

Will anyone rob God?

Yet you are robbing me! But you say, "How are we robbing you?" In your tithes and offerings! You are cursed with a curse, for you are robbing me—the whole nation of you!

Bring the full tithe into the storehouse, so that there may be food in my house, and thus put me to the test, says the Lord of hosts; see if I will not open the windows of heaven for you and pour down for you an overflowing blessing.

After experiencing what it was like to have God open the windows of heaven and pour into my life an overflowing blessing, I decided to give tithing a try.

I also wanted to incorporate some get-rich-quick strategies that I had been learning about from a financial seminar. The seminar leader said that everybody needed to have a goal concerning the amount of money they wanted to earn in a year.

Instead of setting a goal to earn $10,000, I set a goal to tithe $1,000, hoping that God would bless my endeavors according to Luke 6:38, which says, *"Give, and it will be given to you. A good measure, pressed down, shaken together, running over, will be put into your lap; for the measure you give will be the measure you get back."*

My plan to earn $10,000 included Don, the public insurance adjuster. After he helped me acquire a better settlement on the rental property, we developed a close friendship. It didn't take long before we made plans to buy late-model insurance salvage vehicles for pennies on the dollar. It was our intention to have the cars repaired, sell them, and split the profits.

Don had a lot of experience evaluating wrecked cars, and it had always been his dream to rebuild insurance salvage vehicles, so we started this endeavor by visiting an auction. To my surprise, there were more than five hundred wrecked cars inside a huge fenced-in lot. All the cars had orange spray-painted numbers on their windshields. Most of the cars had been involved in front-end collisions or roll-over accidents. The cars that appeared to be in good condition had generally been involved in some kind of flood or theft loss.

We submitted written bids on several vehicles,

and within a few days, we were awarded our first car. After having the vehicle repaired at a nearby body shop, I ran an ad in the newspaper and sold it for a substantial profit. After I shared half the proceeds with Don, we went back to the auction to find more deals.

It didn't take long before we opened an eighteen-bay body shop that specialized in the repair of vehicles that were involved in roll-over accidents. We learned some painful lessons on the first few cars we bought that had been involved in front-end collisions—not realizing they would require a lot of expensive mechanical parts. To repair the roll-over vehicles, all we needed to do was jack up the roof and replace a few pieces of sheet metal. After repainting the cars, we were able to sell them at a huge discount and still make a great profit.

During this time, I was able to make my tithing goals. Year after year, I kept increasing the amount of money that I wanted to give to God, and every year God blessed my efforts to the point where my annual income always exceeded my proposed goal. When I made a commitment to tithe $3,000, my income exceeded $30,000. When I made a commitment to tithe $5,000, my income exceeded $50,000 that year.

At the height of the car business I was selling a car a week and making more than $1,000 per vehicle. Although I had a great time driving a different car around every week, deep in my heart I felt a conflict of interest. Part of me wanted to be a godly man, a man of integrity, a man after God's own heart, but there was another part that I didn't like very much—the part of a used-car salesman.

Even worse than being a used-car salesman, I was selling insurance salvage to unsuspecting buyers. The conflict occurred because nobody wanted to buy a wrecked car. In order to sell the cars, I operated in a gray area otherwise known as lying. Instead of disclosing the truth about the vehicles, I usually told the buyers that we had made a few cosmetic repairs and repainted the entire vehicle, so that it would look like a brand-new car.

After closing the body shop and parting ways with Don, I started buying condemned HUD houses. Renovating dilapidated real estate felt a lot more ethical than selling wrecked cars, because it provided a service to the neighborhood and helped increase my neighbors' property values. Most of the houses I bought had been used as gang hangouts. The roofs had been leaking for years, and the hardwood floors were buckled. It wasn't unusual to find the kitchens stripped clean. On one property, all the cabinets were missing, and the only thing left were a few pipes protruding from the wall.

Selling the homes after they had been renovated brought in a lot more money than the cars. Because the savings and loans were going through a great deal of turnover during that time, I was able to buy the houses between $8,000 and $15,000. After spending $5,000 to $8,000 in construction costs, I was able to sell the houses for a $20,000 profit.

Year after year, I continued to make my tithing goals. When I made a commitment to tithe $10,000, God blessed my business endeavors to the point where I made more than $100,000. When I made a commitment to tithe $20,000, God blessed my efforts, allowing me to make more than $200,000.

Eventually, the inventory of foreclosed homes started to decline, and I could no longer buy properties for pennies on the dollar. Because the price of real estate was on the rise, I started looking for land. Having spent the last five years of my life renovating dusty, older homes, the idea of getting into new construction sounded cleaner and a lot more profitable.

CHAPTER THREE

I was able to find a townhouse development located on a beautiful golf course for only $40,000. It had a great view of the fourth fairway and was surrounded by red rock formations, tall native grass, and scrub oak.

The previous builder had declared bankruptcy because he couldn't sell any of the units. The foundation for the second building had already been poured. The tap fees had been paid. The underground utilities for the water, sewer, and electrical had already been installed. All I needed to do was install a gas line, pave the road, and build the units.

I worked on the project for a little more than two years, and upon its completion, I considered myself financially retired. I was twenty-eight years old, and in my last year of business I had grossed more than $1,200,000. I was able to make my tithing goal for the year in excess of $50,000. All I needed to do was invest my money in the stock market, and I could live off the interest for the rest of my life.

After selling my backhoe, lumber truck, and skid loader, I started praying for a way to use my money trading the markets so that I could give God an even greater offering. Time and time again, God had poured forth his abundant blessings into my life. God had been so good to me that I wanted to give back more, so I started wondering what would happen if I gave God a 38 percent offering on all my stock market trades.

If I gave God 38 percent (which would be more than I would have to pay in taxes), then thousands of people's lives could be changed for the better. The more I thought about taking money from rich Wall Street bankers and giving it to the poor, the more excited I became about trading the markets.

After thinking about the eternal benefits of helping thousands of people, I began working on a trading system. I started by researching several years of market data and even bought a subscription to the fastest real-time data delivery system. Eventually, I was able to develop an indicator that gave me a daily signal whether to go long or short. The system worked great on paper, averaging more than a 300 percent return.

When I started trading the system with real money, the emotional dynamics of fear and greed started to influence my decisions. Within the first few weeks, I was up $10,000, but then the market turned against me. At first the loss didn't seem real because it was only a negative number on the computer screen. The loss would only become real if I sold my position. Because I didn't want to accept the loss, I decided to hold my position until the market turned around.

Every day, I would get up in the morning and stare at the computer screen until the market closed. It was making me sick to watch my loss grow by the thousands. Before long, I couldn't eat or sleep. I was falling deeper into depression.

Then one day I realized I had been trading in denial. The loss was real, and according to the momentum of the market, it didn't look like it would ever turn around. As some point I needed to close my position and accept the consequences of losing more than a quarter of a million dollars.

I was devastated. It felt like I had just lost all the years of my life that I had spent acquiring the money. All the times I had fought to save ten cents on a board foot of siding had been spent in vain. All the money I had saved by paying my employees the smallest amount possible, while trying to extract the maximum amount of work from them, had all disappeared with a flash on the trading platform.

I continued to beat myself up until I couldn't take it any longer. It felt like my life was destroyed. I needed help, but no one could understand what I was going through. Not knowing what to do, I made an appointment to see my pastor.

At the time, Father Bill was serving at the cathedral. After the receptionist led me into his office, he listened very carefully to my story and said, "Why don't you go on retreat?"

"That's a great idea," I said. "After all, it was God

who inspired me with the stock market trading program in the first place!"

After leaving my pastor's office, I went home to pack my bags. The more I thought about my loss, the more angry I became. How dare God allow me to lose all that money! I couldn't wait to get to the retreat center. I was going to have it out with the Almighty on the tallest mountaintop available.

The retreat center was located at the base of a vast mountain range, surrounded by tall pines, running streams, and lush aspen groves. At the entrance of the property, an old stone church had been built on a large rock formation overlooking a small pond. As I drove up the hill toward the main entrance, my attention was fixed on the towering mountain peaks in the distance.

After checking into my room, I laced up my hiking boots, and blasted through the forest like a bulldozer. I crashed my way through trees, across flowing streams, and over large rock formations. Upon reaching the top, I cried out to God for hours, but he was nowhere to be found. When I needed God the most, all I could hear was the sound of the soft mountain breeze.

Eventually, I made my way back to the retreat center, and upon entering my room, I fell facedown on the floor and started crying. I was curled up on the floor, broken and crushed, my life completely destroyed, and from the depths of my being, I surrendered my life unto the Lord. With the unspoken words of my heart I said, "I will do whatever you want from here on out." As soon as I spoke those words, and meant them with every fiber of my being, the presence of the Lord appeared like a bolt of lightning. Instantly, I was flooded with a sense of peace. I arose from the floor with my first assignment—to write a book.

It was a night and day difference. One minute I was broken and crushed, the next, I was filled with peace and joy. The calling to write a book seemed very strange to me, because I had never wanted to write anything. When I was in grade school, my teachers pulled me out of the regular class and put me in a special program called The Reading Center. It was a very humiliating experience to be removed from class with a few other kids who couldn't keep up, and now God was calling me to write a book.

CHAPTER FOUR

I left the retreat center the next day filled with joy thinking the book would be a best seller and that I would get my money back. I worked on the project for almost two years, and during that time, God wanted to do a lot of work on me.

One of the first lessons I learned was that God wanted to work very closely with me on the book project. My first tendency was to act like a little kid who says, "Mine, don't touch." I was planning on putting together three hundred pages of text and submitting it to God when it was finished. Instead, God wanted to establish a deep working relationship with me and open up a better line of communication.

In an attempt to learn how to listen and discern the voice of the Lord, I had to spend a lot of time practicing contemplative prayer. The practice of discerning God's voice from all the other noisy distractions in life occurred deep within my heart. The problem was that my heart was full of all kinds of emotional wounds from the past that God wanted to heal.

I grew up in a good home, but deep in my heart I had a lot of repressed anger toward my parents. One of the chapters in the book was on forgiveness, so it seemed only appropriate that I would spend some time working on my own issues. In an attempt to work through the forgiveness process, I started drafting a healing letter exercise where all the negative emotions were released on paper so that in the second part of the exercise, I could accept more of God's love and forgiveness.

During this time, I wrote more than one hundred healing letters. I wrote forgiveness letters to my parents, schoolteachers, and old girlfriends. Every time I wrote a healing letter, I experienced a deeper encounter with God. The letters were so powerful they invoked tears of love, as the repressed emotions were brought to the surface and healed.

After I had worked on the book for several years, it was finally ready to be released. I spent a lot of money on publicity and marketing, which produced many newspaper articles and radio interviews, but the publicity never seemed to generate enough sales to pay for themselves. After spending over a year trying every possible way to market the book, I began growing a little frustrated with the Lord.

One day, I had been sitting in silence for more than an hour practicing contemplative prayer when I felt an angry part of myself rising up. In my arrogance, I said to the Lord, "Here I am a successful car dealer, body shop owner, and real estate developer, and you have me sitting around all week crying, fasting, and writing healing letters!"

When I surrendered my life into the Lord's service, I meant it with every fiber of my being. Before my stock market loss, I considered myself to be self-employed. I used to live my life any way I wanted, and when I needed something, I would turn to God in prayer. After surrendering my life to the Lord, I became God-employed. In the same way that a servant belongs to his master and is expected to accomplish his master's desires, so too had I surrendered my life into the Lord's service. Whatever the Lord wanted me to do, I would work my hardest to accomplish the task.

From the moment I made my commitment while lying on the retreat house floor, I had been diligently seeking the Lord's will and accomplishing whatever he asked me to do. Now that I had been faithfully following the Lord for almost three years, it felt like my life had been put on hold. I could be out earning hundreds of thousands of dollars, but no, the Lord would rather have me sitting around all day trying to sell a book, in hopes of making a few dollars in profit.

As I continued to grumble against the Lord, I received my next assignment. I didn't hear any audible words, but I knew in my heart that God wanted me to leave everything behind and experience what it would be like to be homeless. After receiving the calling to live on the streets for a few days, I had a decision to make—would I be obedient or pretend I didn't hear him correctly?

A few days later, I dressed in several layers of old warm clothes. I bought an army duffel bag from a thrift store and made a few cardboard signs that said,

Need $6 to eat today, Will work for food, and Honk if you love Jesus. I left my money and cell phone at home, parked my truck at my parents' house, and started walking down West Colfax Avenue.

Upon arriving at the first intersection, I pulled out the sign that said, Need $6 to eat today. I tried to make eye contact with some of the motorists who were stopped at the red light, but no one would even look at me. I held the sign for more than an hour before giving up and sitting down in the grass.

In my discouragement, I turned to the Lord in prayer by saying, "This is going to be a very long and painful weekend." As soon as I started to pray, a woman honked her horn. She was waving cash out her car window, saying, "Do you need money?"

I jumped up and ran across the street. She gave me $6, which allowed me to ride a bus downtown. After walking around for a few hours, I found a church group that had set up tables in an empty parking lot. They were serving hot meals, so I joined the line, and after receiving a plate, I took a seat next to an old man with a long gray beard.

I started a conversation by asking him the locations of the shelters and about other requirements for living on the streets. Even though he offered me a lot of great tips on where to sleep at night, I ended up taking a homeless person home with me that evening. I figured that having love and compassion for the lost was more important than any amount of suffering I would have experienced sleeping outside.

Even though my weekend on the streets didn't

last for more than a day, I learned some extremely valuable lessons. First of all, it taught me humility. I also learned compassion for the homeless. This experience was also the birth of my homeless ministry, because from that point forward, I started going down to the Platte River to minister to those in need.

CHAPTER FIVE
$

One of the things I discovered while working the Platte River was that many of the homeless were addicted to drugs and alcohol. One man named Jim drank a half gallon of vodka a day. He would hold up a cardboard sign near a busy, downtown intersection in order to acquire about $30 a day. He spent some of the money on food and an occasional hotel room, but most nights, he would pass out drunk in the bushes.

As I continued working with the men and women who made their campsites near the river, I discovered that many of them had been married, owned their own homes, and even driven a car to work, but because of their lifelong struggles with drugs and alcohol, many of them had spent their lives in and out of jail and detox facilities. Eventually, they had given up trying to live normal lives and spent their time panhandling and getting high.

Before I started working with the homeless, I thought many of these men and women were just down on their luck or victims of a depressed economy.

There had been many times when I spent my tithing money giving a man a handful of cash, thinking that cash would solve his problems. Unfortunately, when an alcoholic or drug addict receives a large sum of cash, only one thought goes through his mind. It might be in that man's best interest to open a savings account, rent a studio apartment, or invest in some tools, but more often than not, he will spend the money getting high.

Before my stock market loss, I thought I could fix everybody's problems by giving them money. I wanted to make millions of dollars trading commodities, and after giving God 38 percent, I would be able to save the world. What I failed to realize is that there is only one savior of the world, and that is Jesus.

It didn't take very long to realize that what these men and women needed most was a spirit-filled encounter with the risen Lord Jesus Christ. Others needed a lot of emotional healing and deliverance work. They also needed accountability, solid friendships, a good job, and a place to call home. Before a man could rise above the streets, he needed both forms of spiritual and financial support.

It is for this reason that Sacred Scripture requires both forms of giving from all believers. In Matthew 28:19–20, Jesus says, *"Go therefore and make disciples of all nations, baptizing them in the name of the Father and of the Son and of the Holy Spirit, and teaching them to obey everything that I have commanded you."* Along with this required form of spiritual giving, we are also required to provide financial support as per Matthew 5:42, which says, *"Give to everyone who begs from you, and do not refuse anyone who wants to borrow from you."*

The book of James 2:14–17 makes the same point by saying, *"What good is it, my brothers and sisters, if you say you have faith but do not have works? Can faith save you? If a brother or sister is naked and lacks daily food, and one of you says to them, 'Go in peace; keep warm and eat your fill,' and yet you do not supply their bodily needs, what is the good of that? So faith by itself, if it has no works, is dead."*

As my work with the homeless continued, I was able to move from the Platte River to a downtown shelter where I started conducting a weekly church service. With more than 120 men and women attending the service, the needs were overwhelming. On many occasions, I would pour out everything that I had to give and leave totally drained. Not only would I spend my time preaching and developing friendships with the men, but I would also buy pocket-sized Bibles to hand out at service, and at least two or three times a year, I would give everybody a new pair of socks and underwear.

Because the needs of 120 homeless men and women were so overwhelming, I tried reaching out to several affluent churches for help. After speaking at one church located in a prominent part of town, I received $100 to buy a case of Bibles, and at least twenty volunteers signed up to help. I called everybody on the list several times in an attempt to set up appointments to visit the shelter, but no one followed through.

I was hoping two or three Christians could befriend a homeless woman and take her out to lunch, but no one would even show up. Eventually, I gave up trying to call the "volunteers" and started asking a few guys from a men's group to get involved.

At first, the majority of the men seemed very hesitant. The only way I could get them to come was to offer them the opportunity to deliver a sermon, but when they arrived, they were totally unprepared for what they encountered. Not only were most of their messages inappropriate for the audience, but they never wanted to come back.

After realizing the majority of affluent Christians spend a lot of money on gated communities and security systems to keep as far away from the homeless as possible, I came up with an even better idea. If I couldn't get Christians from an affluent church to visit the poor, then maybe I could bring the poor to their church.

CHAPTER SIX

I figured helping a homeless woman would feel less threatening than ministering to a man, so after working with a woman named Amelia for several months, I rented her a hotel room on the south side of town. I asked everybody I knew at that church for help, and only a few people made an effort to reach out to Amelia. One woman offered her a job straightening out the songbooks in the pews after service.

Unfortunately, the majority of the Christians looked at me with disdain. I'm sure others were probably thinking that I was having an affair with her, or some other perverted thought. Amelia could feel the coldness and distance as well. She didn't feel loved or accepted by anyone, and within a few weeks, she decided to go back to living underneath an outdoor billboard sign where she felt safe.

As I wrestled with the reason why so many Christians were unwilling or unprepared to help the poor, I came to the conclusion of bad theology. For many Christians the only requirement to enter into eternal life is for that person to raise their hand during an altar call. These Christians lead lives no different than anyone else in the world, except for maintaining a mental belief that they get to go to heaven.

Other Christians have been condemning good works, as if they were associated with the plague. Many of these Christians like twisting a passage of Scripture out of context from Isaiah 64:6 that says, *"All our righteous acts are like filthy rags."*[1] If they studied the book of Isaiah as it was written for its original audience, they would see that God and Isaiah were having a conversation, and in this passage, Isaiah is making a prayer of repentance on behalf of the nation. No different than if someone were to pray, "O God, please have mercy on America. There's no one who calls on your name. All our good deeds have become like filthy rags."

In the following chapter we see God responding to Isaiah's prayer of repentance, and in no way does God condemn good works. In fact, it's just the opposite. In Isaiah 58:6–8 we see God requiring good works by saying, *"Is not this the fast that I choose: to loose the bonds of injustice, to undo the thongs of the yoke, to let the oppressed go free, and to break every yoke? Is it not to share your bread with the hungry, and bring the homeless poor into your house; when you see the naked, to cover them, and not to hide yourself from your own kin? Then your light shall break forth like the dawn, and your healing shall spring up quickly; your vindicator shall go before you, the glory of the Lord shall be your rear guard."*

Another hindrance that prevents Christians from

reaching out to help the poor comes from a belief that God just wants us to relax and have fun. These Christian will say things like, "Take it easy. Don't work too hard. God wants you to be happy. God wants you to enjoy life." If the proper biblical worldview was to relax, be happy, and enjoy life, then why would anybody want to spend their time helping the homeless?

Another hindrance that prevents Christians from reaching out to the poor comes from the false god of money. In Matthew 6:24 Jesus says, *"No one can serve two masters; for a slave will either hate the one and love the other, or be devoted to the one and despise the other. You cannot serve God and wealth."*

I learned this lesson the hard way. After losing a quarter of a million dollars trading the markets, I realized how I had been serving the false god of money all my life. After I surrendered my life into the Lord's service, I discovered the true meaning of putting the Lord's will first. Instead of working to make money every day, I started working to please the Lord. Instead of trying to acquire a bigger house, the Lord wanted me to sell my house and start serving the homeless. Instead of driving unproductive workers off my jobsite, the Lord wanted me to start driving homeless men around town to look for work.

CHAPTER SEVEN

In my attempt to discover the proper Christian worldview, I had to evaluate my life from an eternal perspective. When most Christians think of our heavenly home, they usually picture themselves sitting around on fluffy white clouds, playing the harp, and singing praises to God. Although this is one possibility, the book of Revelation offers a different perspective. According to Saint John who received the vision, God is going to establish a new heaven and a new earth:

For the first heaven and the first earth had passed away, and the sea was no more. And I saw the holy city, the new Jerusalem, coming down out of heaven from God, prepared as a bride adorned for her husband.[2]

Then the angel said to John, *"Come, I will show you the bride, the wife of the Lamb." And in the spirit he carried me away to a great, high mountain and showed me the holy city Jerusalem coming down out of heaven from God. It has the glory of God and a radiance like a very rare jewel, like jasper, clear as crystal.[3]*

I saw no temple in the city, for its temple is the Lord God the Almighty and the Lamb. And the city has no need of sun or moon to shine on it, for the glory of God is its light, and its lamp is the Lamb. The nations will walk by its light, and the kings of the earth will bring their glory into it. Its gates will never be shut by day—and there will be no night there.[4]

The angel who talked to me had a measuring rod of gold to measure the city and its gates and walls. The city lies foursquare, its length the same as its width; and he measured the city with his rod, fifteen hundred miles; its length and width and height are equal.[5]

According to the angel, the heavenly city is going to be fifteen hundred miles long, fifteen hundred miles wide, and fifteen hundred miles tall. When I looked at a map to see how large a city of that size would be, I calculated it would stretch from New York City to Cuba, from Cuba over to Mexico City, and from Mexico City up to Cheyenne, Wyoming.

In John 14:2–3 Jesus talks about the heavenly kingdom by saying, *"In my Father's house there are many dwelling places. If it were not so, would I have told you that I go to prepare a place for you? And if I go and prepare a place for you, I will come again and will take you to myself, so that where I am, there you may be also."*

The dwelling places that Jesus is talking about are most likely located within the holy city—the new Jerusalem. Because eternity is a very long time, it is possible that God may have his beloved children living in all kinds of different places and accomplishing all kinds of works, but according to Sacred Scripture, this looks like it will be our first destination.

After we pass the test called life, we will be assigned a place in the heavenly kingdom. The servants who use their talents and abilities wisely in this life will be greatly rewarded. Jesus will be the King of all kings and the Lord of all lords in the heavenly kingdom, but he will also assign positions of power to all his followers. According to Luke 19:11–27, once Jesus is seated on the throne of glory, he will call his servants forward to see how they used their talents and abilities:

When the first servant came forward, he said, *"Lord, your pound has made ten more pounds." He said to him, "Well done, good slave! Because you have been trustworthy in a very small thing, take charge of ten cities." Then the second came, saying, "Lord, your pound has made five pounds." He said to him, "And you, rule over five cities."[6]*

The cities that Jesus will assign to his servants are most likely located within the holy city—the new Jerusalem. The servants who pass the test of life will be greatly rewarded in their future home, and those who fail the test will suffer a great loss. A good example of this loss comes from the servant in Matthew 25:14–30 who came forward and said, *"Master, I knew that you were a harsh man, reaping where you did not sow, and gathering where you did not scatter seed; so I was afraid, and I went and hid your talent in the ground. Here you have what is yours."[7]*

But his master replied, *"You wicked and lazy slave! You knew, did you, that I reap where I did not sow, and gather where I did not scatter? Then you ought to have invested my money with the bankers, and on my return I would have received what was my own with interest. So take the talent from him, and give it to the one with the ten talents. As for this worthless slave, throw him into the outer darkness, where there will be weeping and gnashing of teeth."[8]*

If the servant who failed to use his talents and abilities to advance God's kingdom here on earth was treated in such a manner, what do you think will happen to those who spend the Lord's talents on themselves? Can you imagine a man coming forward and saying, "Lord, you gave me ten talents so I used the money to buy a nice house. I lived in luxury every day of my life not thinking twice about my status in your heavenly kingdom."

CHAPTER EIGHT

According to Sacred Scripture, the heavenly kingdom will operate in the exact opposite of our earthly kingdom. If you want to grow rich on earth, you will need to work very hard, charge higher prices, demand a greater return, and take advantage of opportunities, market conditions, employees, and clients.

If you want to grow rich in the heavenly kingdom, you will need to follow the Lord's directive from Luke 12:32–34, where Jesus says, *"Do not be afraid, little flock, for it is your Father's good pleasure to give you the kingdom. Sell your possessions, and give alms. Make purses for yourselves that do not wear out, an unfailing treasure in heaven, where no thief comes near and no moth destroys. For where your treasure is, there your heart will be also."*

If you want to be first in the earthly kingdom, you will need to make a lot of money, wear the latest fashions, and drive a new car. If you want to be first in the heavenly kingdom, you will need to follow the Lord's directive in Matthew 19:28–29, where Jesus says, *"Truly I tell you, at the renewal of all things, when the Son of Man is seated on the throne of his glory, you who have followed me will also sit on twelve thrones, judging the twelve tribes of Israel. And everyone who has left houses or brothers or sisters or father or mother or children or fields, for my name's sake, will receive a hundredfold, and will inherit eternal life."*

Another Scripture passage that points toward our inheritance in the heavenly kingdom comes from the beatitudes, where Jesus says, *"Blessed are the meek, for they will inherit the earth."*[9] The meek in this life are usually the poor, the downtrodden, the elderly, the disabled, and the neglected. The meek don't seem to have very many rights in our modern-day society. When a powerful landlord wants to tear down a tenement to build a shopping center, the meek get evicted. The meek are usually locked away in nursing homes or end up working day labor, because they can't find a steady job.

The only way the meek will inherit the earth is when King Jesus establishes the new heaven and the new earth. On that day, the meek will be given a great inheritance within the fifteen-hundred-mile city, while the rich and powerful in this life might find themselves living in the basement. That is, if they are allowed access at all. According to Matthew 19:23–24, Jesus says, *"Truly I tell you, it will be hard for a rich person to enter the kingdom of heaven. Again I tell you, it is easier for a camel to go through the eye of a needle than for someone who is rich to enter the kingdom of God."*

After realizing that this life is no more than a test that will determine my position in the heavenly kingdom, I decided to start banking as much heavenly treasure as possible. I started this process by acquiring a list of the poorest countries in the world. According to statistics from the United States government, the average American per capita income is $48,000 per year.[10] Some of the poorest countries in the world include places like Zimbabwe, where the average citizen earns less than $1 per day. In Ethiopia, the average citizen earns $2.19 per day, and in Haiti, the average per capita income is $3.84 per day.

Rank	Country	GDP/Per Capita	Date
1	Liechtenstein	$ 118,000	2007 est.
2	Qatar	$ 101,000	2008 est.
3	Luxembourg	$ 85,100	2008 est.
4	Bermuda	$ 69,900	2004 est.
5	Kuwait	$ 60,800	2008 est.
6	Norway	$ 57,500	2008 est.
7	Jersey	$ 57,000	2005 est.
8	Brunei	$ 54,100	2008 est.
9	Singapore	$ 52,900	2008 est.
10	United States	$ 48,000	2008 est.
11	Ireland	$ 47,800	2008 est.
12	San Marino	$ 46,100	2006 est.
13	Hong Kong	$ 45,300	2008 est.
14	Guernsey	$ 44,600	2005 est.
15	Cayman Islands	$ 43,800	2004 est.
16	Iceland	$ 42,600	2008 est.
17	Netherlands	$ 41,300	2008 est.

18	Switzerland	$ 40,900	2008 est.
19	United Arab Emirates	$ 40,400	2008 est.
20	Canada	$ 40,200	2008 est.
21	Austria	$ 39,600	2008 est.
22	Sweden	$ 39,600	2008 est.
23	Australia	$ 39,300	2008 est.
24	Denmark	$ 38,900	2008 est.
25	Andorra	$ 38,800	2005 est.
26	British Virgin Islands	$ 38,500	2004 est.
27	Finland	$ 38,400	2008 est.
28	Belgium	$ 38,300	2008 est.
29	Gibraltar	$ 38,200	2005 est.
30	United Kingdom	$ 37,400	2008 est.
31	Bahrain	$ 37,200	2008 est.
32	Falkland Islands	$ 35,400	2002 est.
33	Japan	$ 35,300	2008 est.
34	Isle of Man	$ 35,000	2005 est.
35	Germany	$ 34,800	2008 est.
36	Spain	$ 34,100	2008 est.
37	European Union	$ 33,800	2008 est.
38	Taiwan	$ 33,000	2008 est.
39	Greece	$ 32,800	2008 est.
40	France	$ 32,700	2008 est.
41	Faroe Islands	$ 31,000	2001 est.
42	Italy	$ 31,000	2008 est.
43	Slovenia	$ 30,800	2008 est.
44	Equatorial Guinea	$ 30,200	2008 est.
45	Monaco	$ 30,000	2006 est.
46	Bahamas, The	$ 29,900	2008 est.
47	Cyprus	$ 29,200	2008 est.
48	Israel	$ 28,900	2008 est.

49	New Zealand	$ 28,500	2008 est.
50	Macau	$ 28,400	2006 est.
51	Trinidad/Tobago	$ 28,400	2008 est.
52	Korea, South	$ 27,100	2008 est.
53	Czech Republic	$ 26,800	2008 est.
54	Malta	$ 24,200	2008 est.
55	Slovakia	$ 22,600	2008 est.
56	Portugal	$ 22,000	2008 est.
57	Estonia	$ 21,900	2008 est.
58	Aruba	$ 21,800	2004 est.
59	Saudi Arabia	$ 21,300	2008 est.
60	Hungary	$ 20,500	2008 est.
61	Oman	$ 20,400	2008 est.
62	Barbados	$ 20,200	2008 est.
63	Greenland	$ 20,000	2001 est.
64	Saint Kitts/Nevis	$ 20,000	2008 est.
65	Antigua/Barbuda	$ 19,100	2008 est.
66	Puerto Rico	$ 18,700	2008 est.
67	Seychelles	$ 18,700	2008 est.
68	Latvia	$ 18,500	2008 est.
69	Lithuania	$ 18,400	2008 est.
70	Poland	$ 17,800	2008 est.
71	French Polynesia	$ 17,500	2003 est.
72	Croatia	$ 16,900	2008 est.
73	Netherlands Antilles	$ 16,000	2004 est.
74	Botswana	$ 15,800	2008 est.
75	Russia	$ 15,800	2008 est.
76	Malaysia	$ 15,700	2008 est.
77	Chile	$ 15,400	2008 est.
78	Guam	$ 15,000	2005 est.
79	New Caledonia	$ 15,000	2003 est.

80	Gabon	$ 14,900	2008 est.
81	Libya	$ 14,900	2008 est.
82	Argentina	$ 14,500	2008 est.
83	Virgin Islands	$ 14,500	2004 est.
84	Mexico	$ 14,400	2008 est.
85	Venezuela	$ 14,000	2008 est.
86	Grenada	$ 13,600	2008 est.
87	Bulgaria	$ 13,200	2008 est.
88	Iran	$ 13,100	2008 est.
89	Turkey	$ 12,900	2008 est.
90	Cuba	$ 12,700	2008 est.
91	Northern Mariana Islands	$ 12,500	2000 est.
92	Romania	$ 12,500	2008 est.
93	Mauritius	$ 12,400	2008 est.
94	Uruguay	$ 12,300	2008 est.
95	Belarus	$ 12,000	2008 est.
96	Kazakhstan	$ 12,000	2008 est.
97	Costa Rica	$ 11,900	2008 est.
98	Panama	$ 11,900	2008 est.
99	Turks/Caicos	$ 11,500	2002 est.
100	Saint Lucia	$ 11,300	2008 est.
101	Lebanon	$ 11,100	2008 est.
102	Montenegro	$ 10,600	2008 est.
103	World	$ 10,500	2008 est.
104	South Africa	$ 10,400	2008 est.
105	Brazil	$ 10,300	2008 est.
106	Azerbaijan	$ 9,500	2008 est.
107	Dominica	$ 9,500	2008 est.
108	Macedonia	$ 9,200	2008 est.
109	Saint Vincent/Grenadines	$ 9,200	2008 est.
110	Angola	$ 9,100	2008 est.

111	Cook Islands	$ 9,100	2005 est.
112	Colombia	$ 9,000	2008 est.
113	Suriname	$ 8,900	2008 est.
114	Anguilla	$ 8,800	2004 est.
115	Dominican Republic	$ 8,800	2008 est.
116	Thailand	$ 8,700	2008 est.
117	Belize	$ 8,500	2008 est.
118	Peru	$ 8,500	2008 est.
119	Serbia	$ 8,200	2008 est.
120	Palau	$ 8,100	2007 est.
121	Tunisia	$ 8,000	2008 est.
122	Ukraine	$ 7,800	2008 est.
123	Ecuador	$ 7,700	2008 est.
124	Jamaica	$ 7,700	2008 est.
125	Algeria	$ 7,100	2008 est.
126	Saint Pierre/Miquelon	$ 7,000	2001 est.
127	Armenia	$ 6,600	2008 est.
128	Bosnia/Herzegovina	$ 6,600	2008 est.
129	Albania	$ 6,400	2008 est.
130	El Salvador	$ 6,400	2008 est.
131	China	$ 6,100	2008 est.
132	American Samoa	$ 5,800	2005 est.
133	Turkmenistan	$ 5,800	2008 est.
134	Niue	$ 5,800	2003 est.
135	Egypt	$ 5,500	2008 est.
136	Namibia	$ 5,500	2008 est.
137	Guatemala	$ 5,400	2008 est.
138	Swaziland	$ 5,100	2008 est.
139	Georgia	$ 5,000	2008 est.
140	Jordan	$ 5,000	2008 est.
141	Nauru	$ 5,000	2005 est.

142	Samoa	$ 5,000	2008 est.
143	Mayotte	$ 4,900	2005 est.
144	Syria	$ 4,900	2008 est.
145	Bhutan	$ 4,800	2008 est.
146	Bolivia	$ 4,700	2008 est.
147	Vanuatu	$ 4,700	2008 est.
148	Maldives	$ 4,500	2008 est.
149	Sri Lanka	$ 4,400	2008 est.
150	Tonga	$ 4,400	2008 est.
151	Paraguay	$ 4,300	2008 est.
152	Cape Verde	$ 4,200	2008 est.
153	Guyana	$ 4,000	2008 est.
154	Morocco	$ 4,000	2008 est.
155	Iraq	$ 4,000	2008 est.
156	Indonesia	$ 3,900	2008 est.
157	Republic of Congo	$ 3,800	2008 est.
158	Djibouti	$ 3,800	2008 est.
159	Wallis/Futuna	$ 3,800	2004 est.
160	Fiji	$ 3,700	2008 est.
161	Honduras	$ 3,700	2008 est.
162	Kiribati	$ 3,700	2008 est.
163	Montserrat	$ 3,400	2002 est.
164	Philippines	$ 3,400	2008 est.
165	Mongolia	$ 3,300	2008 est.
166	Nicaragua	$ 3,000	2008 est.
167	Gaza Strip	$ 2,900	2008 est.
168	West Bank	$ 2,900	2008 est.
169	Vietnam	$ 2,900	2008 est.
170	Marshall Islands	$ 2,900	2005 est.
171	India	$ 2,900	2008 est.
172	Uzbekistan	$ 2,700	2008 est.

173	Pakistan	$ 2,600	2008 est.
174	Yemen	$ 2,600	2008 est.
175	Moldova	$ 2,500	2008 est.
176	Saint Helena	$ 2,500	1998 est.
177	Timor-Leste	$ 2,500	2008 est.
178	Cameroon	$ 2,400	2008 est.
179	Micronesia	$ 2,300	2005 est.
180	Papua New Guinea	$ 2,300	2008 est.
181	Kyrgyzstan	$ 2,200	2008 est.
182	Nigeria	$ 2,200	2008 est.
183	Sudan	$ 2,200	2008 est.
184	Cambodia	$ 2,100	2008 est.
185	Laos	$ 2,100	2008 est.
186	Solomon Islands	$ 1,900	2008 est.
187	Mauritania	$ 1,900	2008 est.
188	Kenya	$ 1,800	2008 est.
189	Korea, North	$ 1,800	2008 est.
190	Tajikistan	$ 1,800	2008 est.
191	Senegal	$ 1,800	2008 est.
192	Kosovo	$ 1,800	2007 est.
193	Cote d'Ivoire	$ 1,700	2008 est.
194	Chad	$ 1,600	2008 est.
195	Lesotho	$ 1,600	2008 est.
196	Tuvalu	$ 1,600	2002 est.
197	Bangladesh	$ 1,500	2008 est.
198	Ghana	$ 1,500	2008 est.
199	Benin	$ 1,500	2008 est.
200	Zambia	$ 1,500	2008 est.
201	Haiti	$ 1,400	2008 est.
202	Tanzania	$ 1,400	2008 est.
203	Sao Tome/Principe	$ 1,400	2008 est.

204	Burkina Faso	$ 1,300	2008 est.
205	Burma	$ 1,200	2008 est.
206	Mali	$ 1,200	2008 est.
207	The Gambia	$ 1,200	2008 est.
208	Comoros	$ 1,100	2008 est.
209	Madagascar	$ 1,100	2008 est.
210	Guinea	$ 1,100	2008 est.
211	Uganda	$ 1,100	2008 est.
212	Nepal	$ 1,000	2008 est.
213	Tokelau	$ 1,000	1993 est.
214	Mozambique	$ 900	2008 est.
215	Togo	$ 900	2008 est.
216	Rwanda	$ 900	2008 est.
217	Afghanistan	$ 800	2008 est.
218	Malawi	$ 800	2008 est.
219	Ethiopia	$ 800	2008 est.
220	Central African Republic	$ 700	2008 est.
221	Niger	$ 700	2008 est.
222	Sierra Leone	$ 700	2008 est.
223	Eritrea	$ 700	2008 est.
224	Guinea-Bissau	$ 600	2008 est.
225	Somalia	$ 600	2008 est.
226	Liberia	$ 500	2008 est.
227	Burundi	$ 400	2008 est.
228	Republic of Congo	$ 300	2008 est.
229	Zimbabwe	$ 200	2008 est.

After looking at this list, I could see that the top-ten nations of the world were extremely rich compared to the poorest countries. Because the United States is listed in the top-ten countries, it gives all Americans a great opportunity to earn a vast amount of heavenly treasure, because of the U.S. dollar's strength in these underdeveloped nations.

For example, a $20 donation to a church in Luxembourg might not go very far. The cost of living in Luxembourg would be considered high compared to American standards, and $20 might not even buy a family of four a meal at a restaurant. At the opposite extreme, a $20 donation to a church in Zimbabwe would go a long way in accomplishing a lot of good. If the average person in Zimbabwe lives on less than $1 per day, then a $20 donation would be enough to feed at least twenty starving people in that country.

CHAPTER NINE

$

In my attempt to understand how a family in Zimbabwe lives on less than $1 per day, I came across a book entitled *Material World*. The photographers who worked on the project traveled the globe taking pictures of average families along with all their household possessions.

The portrait that best represents the average American household comes from Texas. The family that was chosen for the profile lives in a sixteen hundred square-foot brick ranch home, owns two cars, and is raising two children. Before the picture was taken, all the family's personal property was set up on display in the street so that everybody could see how the average American lives.

As you can imagine, this family owns the typical kitchen appliances. They have two television sets, five telephones, four bicycles, and a desktop computer. The children have their own bedroom sets complete with a bed, nightstand, dresser, and lots of toys. The family also owns a dune buggy, a piano, and the typical living and dining room furniture.

At the opposite extreme, the average family in Mali lives in a 540 square-foot home made out of adobe bricks. From the photograph, it looks like the family built the house themselves by covering the structure with clay. The majority of the family's possessions consist of a few cooking pots and baskets. The father owns a bicycle and works 112 hours a week to earn $251 per year. There's no running water or electricity at the property. To wash clothes, the family with six children uses a metal tub, and afterward they dry the laundry on sticks near an open fire pit, which is also used for cooking.

A family with five children from Ethiopia lives in a 320 square-foot wooden shack made out of tree branches. The inside walls are lined with cattle dung that has been mixed with straw to make a type of plaster. The father works eighty hours a week to earn $123 per year as a farmer. His most valuable possession is a team of oxen, which he uses to plow a field in an attempt to grow grain to feed his family.

11

As I looked at the other portraits from around the world, I realized that just being grateful that I'm an American would not be enough. The Lord has given me many different talents and abilities, and one day I will have to stand before him to render an account. I had already surrendered my life into his service and now that I was committed to earning as much heavenly treasure as possible, I knew that some type of action was required.

Not knowing where to begin the journey, I booked a flight to Ghana. My first stop was the capital city of Accra. Even though it was the most developed city in the nation, there were open sewers running through town. The majority of the roads were not paved and were riddled with potholes. The residents who lived near the ocean used rock formations along the beach as a public bathroom. I saw a herd of pigs eating out of a trash dump that was located fifteen feet away from the beach. There was garbage all over the place, severe air pollution, chickens that had been marked with spray paint, and stray dogs with tumors wandering around.

During my visit, I had the opportunity to speak at a church located in an automobile repair district. All the wooden shacks on that block operated some type of repair service, and they all had used-car parts scattered all over the place. There were axles from buses and tires from dump trucks lying on the ground which was saturated with oil and grease from where the mechanics had worked on their clients' vehicles.

At the end of the automobile repair district was another wooden shack that served as a church. When

I arrived for my speaking engagement, the door was secured with a heavy chain and a padlock. Because I had arrived a half hour early, I took the opportunity to walk around. There was a large open field behind the church that the neighborhood used for a trash dump. After taking a closer look, I noticed little kids rummaging through the garbage.

I was so excited to be able to minister to kids who were living in a trash dump that I walked out into the field to get closer. When the children saw me, they huddled together in a tight cluster. I tried talking to them, but my attempt to communicate only seemed to frighten them. When I tried moving closer, they started to run, so I stopped and took a picture before heading back to the church.

When the pastor arrived I said, "There's little naked kids out there in the trash dump."

"I know," the pastor said. "We are hoping to build a fence to keep the trash away from our property."

"What about the kids?" I asked.

He just looked at me with a blank stare on his face. It was apparent that although they numbered in the thousands, little children in Africa were not very important. Especially, if they were from poor, uneducated families who were living in the trash dump. I tried to talk with him about the importance of little children from God's perspective, but before long, the entire congregation had gathered, and it was time to start the service.

When it came time to deliver my message, all I could do was think about the poor little kids. Half the congregation didn't speak English, so the pastor stood next to me with a microphone in an attempt to translate. By the way he was looking at me, I'm not sure whether he liked what I was saying, or maybe he just didn't understand, so halfway through the sermon, I changed the topic and shared with the congregation my desire to help the kids who were living in the dump.

To do this, I offered to pay for a community dinner. I envisioned several women cooking a great feast. After the entire congregation had invited all of their auto mechanic neighbors to join the celebration, the pastor could offer a teaching about Jesus and pray to bless the meal. It seemed like a great way for the church to reach out to the community and also minister to the kids in the trash dump.

The vision for the community dinner was so clear, but I'm not sure anyone in the congregation understood what I was talking about. Everybody seemed excited that I was offering their church financial support, but after I give the pastor several hundred dollars for the community dinner, he later sent me pictures that looked like the church had just thrown a big party for themselves.

I tried working with this pastor for several more months, and it turns out he spent most of the money on his associate pastors' salaries. I also gave him $100 to buy Bibles, and he only bought two. Judging from the pictures he sent me, they looked like used Bibles in poor condition.

CHAPTER TEN

$

Even though I was greatly disappointed by this pastor's actions and lack of concern for the poor, I continued searching for other churches in Africa who would share the same vision. Deep in my heart I knew this was the best way to earn the greatest amount of heavenly treasure from a very small investment. All I needed to do was find the right church and make sure that I gave them very clear and detailed instructions.

I started my search by contacting several dioceses in Tanzania to ask if they knew of anybody who cared for the poor. After receiving the name of a children's home who supported fifty-six orphans, I sent the sister in charge several $100 checks. After cashing the checks at the local bank, the sister was only able to buy a little milk for the kids. Part of the problem was that the sister didn't realize that one hundred U.S. dollars was equivalent to 134,300 Tanzanian shillings. The other part of the problem was that the bankers charged her an exorbitant amount of fees to cash and convert a U.S. bank draft.

To solve this problem, I opened several checking accounts, along with corresponding ATM cards, at a bank where I had no other previous dealings. After sending the ATM cards to charitable organizations, they would be able to use them to withdraw funds from the account. Because ATM cards offer some of the best exchange rates and the lowest fees, this option sounded like the most economical way to send money to Africa.

The risk of opening a bank account at an institution where all my other accounts were located is that bankers have a tendency to link all their customer accounts together. They also like to issue credit cards and overdraft protection. When I opened an account for a pastor in Africa, I had to make sure there was no way for him to overdraw the account, get access to my other accounts, or make any purchases on credit. Once the bank account was opened and the ATM card issued, I could deposit $100 into a pastor's account, and he could withdraw the funds the same day.

After opening several charity accounts, I met a pastor from Nigeria who also shared the same vision in regard to helping the poor. I asked him to choose seven women from his congregation who would prepare the food. The women were to meet together and pray for the program and for the poor in their community. Once the women developed a strong ministry team, I sent the pastor the ATM card with specific instructions, "The money is only to be used to buy food for the poor. You are not allowed to use the money to buy gas for your car, to pay your cell phone bill, or to spend it on yourself."

When the pastor from Nigeria agreed to the specific terms, I sent him the password. Because he lived in a rural area, he had a hard time finding a bank that was connected to the MasterCard/Cirrus network, but after I helped him use an online locator, he was able to withdraw the money. Even though I had deposited a little more than $100 into his account, I gave him specific instructions that he was only to withdraw 12,000 Nigerian naira on the first day of the month.

As soon as the pastor received the money, he gave it to the women, who bought food to prepare the community dinner. On the first Sunday of the month, his entire congregation conducted an outdoor service in the park. Members from his community went out into the neighborhood to invite the poor, disabled, and elderly. When a large crowd gathered the pastor proclaimed the good news about God's extravagant love. He shared the Gospel message and prayed for healing with all those who were sick. Then the food was served.

Little kids who had been living in extreme poverty came with their parents to receive an incredible banquet. Soon, the word spread throughout the region. After seeing and experiencing the love of Christ, people started joining his church. The pastor reported a 30 percent increase in his congregation. Every Sunday there were more people coming to hear the word of God. After increasing the pastor's monthly allowance to 15,000 Nigerian naira per month, the women's food program continues to grow in strength and prosperity.

CHAPTER ELEVEN

In my excitement to set up a vast number of food programs throughout Africa, I failed to conduct a thorough background check on one pastor from the Ivory Coast. This man contacted me by e-mail asking for Bibles, and from his correspondence, he sounded like a genuine and sincere pastor. All his messages were filled with religious-sounding greetings that invoked the name of Christ.

When I asked him to take a picture of his congregation holding up the Bibles and prayer books that I had sent, he complied with the request and sent a photograph of a church service with several men holding up the prayer booklets. As it turns out, the man was a con artist who falsified documents and spent the food program money on what he claimed to be his own "housing problem." I had worked with this man for more than a year, when he finally confessed to lying and setting up fake e-mail accounts, which he used while pretending to be someone else.

Although Africa is a great place to earn a vast

amount of heavenly treasure, it is also a place filled with con artists and cleverly disguised scams. It is not enough to call a man on his cell phone or send correspondence to a post office box when verifying a pastor's authenticity. I now have a new policy whereby every pastor I work with needs to be verified through a neutral third party. If a pastor is genuine, he should be able to produce several letters of reference from local government officials or from other churches in the area.

Once I receive a letter of reference, I verify the source to make sure it is authentic. On one occasion, I received two letters of reference from a pastor in Kenya. One letter was from a Catholic priest, and the other from the village chief. In the letterhead from the priest, the word diocese was misspelled, which made me very suspicious.

In order to verify the source, I had to contact the Catholic diocese and speak to the bishop to make sure the priest who wrote the letter was real. As it turns out, the letter was authentic. The pastor from Kenya has a deep love for the orphans and street kids who have lost their parents to AIDS or because of post-election violence. Because there is a severe lack of food, accommodations, clothing, and educational opportunities for the street kids, the pastor from Kenya continues to search the city every week for abandoned kids, so he can bring them into his orphanage.

It would be nice if there were a spiritual indicator letting me know how much heavenly treasure the African pastors were producing. With our modern-day technology, there are brokerage account indicators that allow investors to see the value of their assets during the fluctuating market conditions. When the Dow Jones Industrial Average goes up a hundred points, the value of the investor's account reflects the increase instantaneously.

In the same way, it would be nice to see how much heavenly treasure the pastor from Kenya is producing, compared with the man from the Ivory Coast. If a $100 investment with the Kenyan pastor was reaping $1,000 in heavenly treasure, compared with a $100 loss from the Ivory Coast con artist, it would be very easy to determine where to invest my money in an attempt to produce the greatest amount of heavenly treasure possible.

Maybe the best way to make sure your hard-earned money is being spent wisely is to accomplish the ministry assignments yourself. That way you will be assured every cent of the Lord's tithing money is producing the greatest amount of wealth for the kingdom of God.

CHAPTER TWELVE

Change Your Worldview

The process of producing the greatest amount of heavenly treasure begins by changing your worldview. In Revelation 22:12 Jesus says, *"See, I am coming soon; my reward is with me, to repay according to everyone's work."* The only thing that truly matters in this life is what you can take with you into eternity. If you have been spending the majority of your time chasing after the American Dream, you might want to ask God to change your perspective.

Make a List of Your Gifts

There are as many different spiritual gifts as there are people who use them. In Exodus 31:3–5, a man by the name of Bezalel was filled with a *divine spirit, with ability, intelligence, and knowledge in every kind of craft, to devise artistic designs, to work in gold, silver, and bronze, in cutting stones for setting, and in carving wood, in every kind of craft.*

1 Corinthians 12:8–10 offers another list of

spiritual gifts: *To one is given through the Spirit the utterance of wisdom, and to another the utterance of knowledge according to the same Spirit, to another faith by the same Spirit, to another gifts of healing by the one Spirit, to another the working of miracles, to another prophecy, to another the discernment of spirits.* In order to use your gifts to their greatest potential, it will be helpful to prayerfully discern the types of gifts that you have been given. Once you know your gifts, it would be helpful to make a list of all the ways you are currently using them and another list of all the ways you can increase your efforts.

Start Producing Heavenly Treasure

In Matthew 6:19–21 Jesus encourages his followers to earn as much heavenly treasure as possible by saying, *"Do not store up for yourselves treasures on earth, where moth and rust consume and where thieves break in and steal; but store up for yourselves treasures in heaven, where neither moth nor rust consumes and where thieves do not break in and steal. For where your treasure is, there your heart will be also."* Heavenly treasure is permanent. The work that you do advancing the kingdom of heaven will last forever, especially when it is combined with the gift of love.

Use Poverty to Your Advantage

It would appear that the poor have a greater advantage over the rich when it comes to producing heavenly treasure. A good example of this comes from Mark 12:41–44, where Jesus *watched the crowd putting money into the treasury. Many rich people put in large sums. A poor widow came and put in two small copper coins, which are worth a penny. Then he called his disciples and said to them, "Truly I tell you, this poor widow has put in more than all those who are contributing to the treasury. For all of them have contributed out of their abundance; but she out of her poverty has put in everything she had, all she had to live on."* From this passage, we can discern that the poor widow's mite earned a greater rate of return on her investment than the largest sums given by the wealthiest men in the synagogue.

Earn the Greatest Rate of Return

Taking a homeless person out to lunch will produce a greater rate of return on your investment than handing out cash, because during this time you will have the opportunity to talk with your guest about Jesus. Anytime a homeless person asks me for a buck, I respond by saying, "I don't give out money, but if you are hungry, I will take you out to lunch." If the man is truly hungry, he will take me up on the offer. But if he starts to grumble and complain by saying, "Lunch! I would rather have the cash!" Then it is a good indicator that the man just wants to use the money for drugs or alcohol. If donating $10 to a shelter nets $10 of eternal wealth, then spending $10 on lunch with a homeless person may be worth ten times that amount in heavenly treasure.

Make Sure You Are Giving Wisely

Producing heavenly treasure is a lot like investing in the stock market. Both endeavors require wisdom and research to be successful. People don't just throw cash around on the trading floor hoping that everything they buy will go up in value. Successful investing requires a long-term approach, a lot of research, and good communication with your broker. In the same way, producing heavenly treasure requires good communication with the Lord Jesus. It will be necessary to spend a lot of time in prayer to discern the best use of your time, talents, and treasure so that you can earn the maximum rate of return on all your investments.

Build on the Foundation of Christ

Just because someone donates money to a non-profit organization doesn't mean they will receive a reward. A good example of our need to build on the foundation of Christ comes from 1 Corinthians 3:10–15, where Saint Paul says, *"Like a skilled master builder I laid a foundation, and someone else is building on it. Each builder must choose with care how to build on it. For no one can lay any foundation other than the one that has been laid; that foundation is Jesus Christ. Now if anyone builds on the foundation with gold, silver, precious stones, wood, hay, straw—the work of each builder will become visible, for the Day will disclose it, because it will be revealed with fire, and the fire will test what sort of work each has done. If what has been built on the foundation survives, the builder will receive a reward. If the work is burned up, the builder will suffer loss."*

A good way to build on the foundation of Christ is by supporting missionaries, providing Bibles to Third-World countries, or by making donations to charitable organizations that proclaim the Gospel message. Those who donate money to political organizations might not receive any reward, and those who support apostate organizations who cause divisions and heresies within the Church, might even experience a loss.

Give Your Best to God

Sacred Scripture offers many examples about our need to give our best to God. In the book of Malachi, the priests were offering unacceptable sacrifices upon the altar, so God confronted them by saying, *"When you offer blind animals in sacrifice, is that not wrong? And when you offer those that are lame or sick, is that not wrong? Try presenting that to your governor; will he be pleased with you or show you favor? says the Lord of hosts. Oh, that someone among you would shut the temple doors, so that you would not kindle fire on my altar in vain! I have no pleasure in you, says the Lord of hosts, and I will not accept an offering from your hands. Cursed be the cheat who has a male in the flock and vows to give it, and yet sacrifices to the Lord what is blemished; for I am a great King, says the Lord of hosts, and my name is reverenced among the nations."*[13] The next time you present an offering before the Lord, whether it be in the church collection basket, or by making a donation to missionaries in India, make sure that you are giving your best to God.

Give to God from a Loving Heart

According to 2 Corinthians 9:6–8, *The one who sows sparingly will also reap sparingly, and the one who sows bountifully will also reap bountifully. Each of you must give as you have made up your mind, not reluctantly or under compulsion, for God loves a cheerful giver. And God is able to provide you with every blessing in abundance, so that by always having enough of everything, you may share abundantly in every good work.*

The proper attitude when giving to God is love. When we give to God we are acknowledging that everything in this world belongs to him, but even more importantly, we are saying thank you for your abundant blessings. When we give to God from a loving heart, it touches God's heart, and in return he wants to increase our blessings. It is for this reason that tithing is nothing more than a mutual exchange of love.

Pray To Be More Productive

When Christians are authentically connected to Christ, they will naturally bear fruit for the kingdom of heaven. A good explanation of this teaching comes from the book of John, where Jesus says, *"I am the true vine, and my Father is the vinegrower. He removes every branch in me that bears no fruit. Every branch that bears fruit he prunes to make it bear more fruit. Abide in me as I abide in you. Just as the branch cannot bear fruit by itself unless it abides in the vine, neither can you unless you abide in me. I am the vine, you are the branches. Those who abide in me and I in them bear much fruit, because apart from me you can do nothing. Whoever does not abide in me is thrown away like a branch and withers; such branches are gathered, thrown into the fire, and burned."[14]*

In this analogy, there are only two options: You are either connected to Jesus in such a way that you are producing fruit for the kingdom of heaven, or you have been cut off from the vine. For those branches that are connected to the vine, the Father prunes to make them bear more fruit. The question that needs to be asked is: How has God the Father been pruning your life to make you bear more fruit? Is there anything in your life that God is calling you to part ways with, so that you can be more productive? If so, you might want to ask your heavenly Father to remove it quickly, so that you can produce the greatest amount of heavenly treasure for the kingdom of God.

Foreword by Most Reverend Philip A S Anyolo, Bishop of Homa Bay Diocese in Kenya, East Africa. If you would like to establish a ministry program with a church in Kenya, please contact the Diocese of Homa Bay for more information: www.catholicdioceseofhomabay.org

1. Isaiah 64:6 from the Holy Bible, New International Version.® Copyright © 1973, 1978, 1984 by International Bible Society. Used by permission of International Bible Society.

2. Revelation 21:1–2.

3. Revelation 21:9–11.

4. Revelation 21:22–25.

5. Revelation 21:15–16.

6. Luke 19:16–19.

7. Matthew 25:24–25.

8. Matthew 25:26–28 & 30.

9. Matthew 5:5.

10. The estimated per capita income has been calculated by the value of all goods and services produced within a country, divided by that country's population. The list has been prepared by the United States Government, Central Intelligence Agency. For

more information please visit: https://www.cia.gov/library/publications/the-world-factbook/rankorder/2004rank.html

11. Photograph of the Natomo family residence from Mali. *Material World: A Global Family Portrait* (San Francisco, CA: Sierra Club Books, 1994), p. 15.

12. Photograph of the Getu family residence from Ethiopia. *Material World: A Global Family Portrait* (San Francisco, CA: Sierra Club Books, 1994), p. 29.

13. Malachi 1:8, 10 & 14.

14. John 15:1–2 & 4–6.

About the Author

Robert Abel's purpose and passion in life is speaking God's truth unto today's generation. He lives in Denver, Colorado, where he leads a homeless ministry and conducts mission trips to Africa.

If you would like to join Robert on the next mission trip, or would like him to speak at your parish, please contact:

www.AfricaMissionaries.com

If you would like to participate in our stewardship ministry, please consider spreading the message from *Heavenly Treasure*. To purchase additional copies of this book for ministry purposes, or to make a donation, please use the following information:

Number of Copies	Ministry Price
6	$29
12	$49
18	$69

These prices include tax and shipping within the United States. For shipments to other countries, please contact us. Thank you for your generous support.

Mail your payment to:

Valentine Publishing House
Heavenly Treasure
P.O. Box 27422
Denver, Colorado 80227